Mom's
Daily Bread

365 SCRIPTURES TO
ENCOURAGE A
MOTHER'S HEART

GOOD BOOKS

Good Books

New York, New York

Good Books books may be purchased in bulk at special discounts for sales promotion, corporate gifts, fund-raising, or educational purposes. Special editions can also be created to specifications. For details, contact the Special Sales Department, Good Books, 307 West 36th Street, 11th Floor, New York, NY 10018 or info@skyhorsepublishing.com.

Good Books is an imprint of Skyhorse Publishing, Inc.®, a Delaware corporation.

Visit our website at www.goodbooks.com.

10 9 8 7 6 5 4 3

Library of Congress Cataloging-in-Publication Data is available on file.

Print ISBN: 978-1-68099-440-7
Ebook ISBN: 978-1-68099-442-1

Cover design by Abigail Gehring
Cover illustration: iStockphoto

Printed in China

Scriptures are taken from the KING JAMES VERSION (KJV), public domain.

For all the mothers—may you be blessed, encouraged,
and challenged by the Word of God.

Take therefore no thought for
the morrow: for the morrow
shall take thought for the
things of itself. Sufficient unto
the day is the evil thereof.

—Matthew 6:34

Verily I say unto you,
Whosoever shall not
receive the kingdom of
God as a little child shall
in no wise enter therein.

—Luke 18:17

It is of the Lord's mercies

that we are not consumed,

because his compassions fail not.

They are new every morning:

great is thy faithfulness.

—Lamentations 3:22-23

Be careful for nothing;
but in every thing by
prayer and supplication
with thanksgiving let
your requests be made
known unto God.

—Philippians 4:6

For thou, LORD, hast made me glad through thy work: I will triumph in the works of thy hands.

–Psalm 92:4

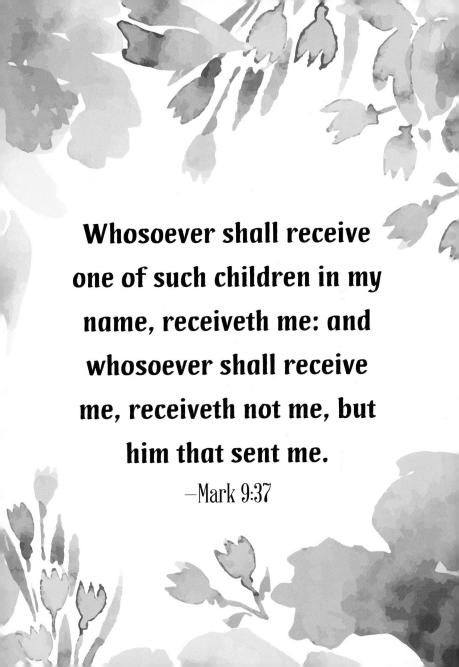

Whosoever shall receive one of such children in my name, receiveth me: and whosoever shall receive me, receiveth not me, but him that sent me.

–Mark 9:37

And these words, which I command thee this day, shall be in thine heart: And thou shalt teach them diligently unto thy children, and shalt talk of them when thou sittest in thine house, and when thou walkest by the way, and when thou liest down, and when thou risest up.

–Deuteronomy 6:6-7

I the Lord have called thee in righteousness, and will hold thine hand, and will keep thee, and give thee for a covenant of the people, for a light of the Gentiles . . .

—Isaiah 42:6

Lo, children are an heritage
of the Lord: and the fruit of
the womb is his reward.

–Psalm 127:3

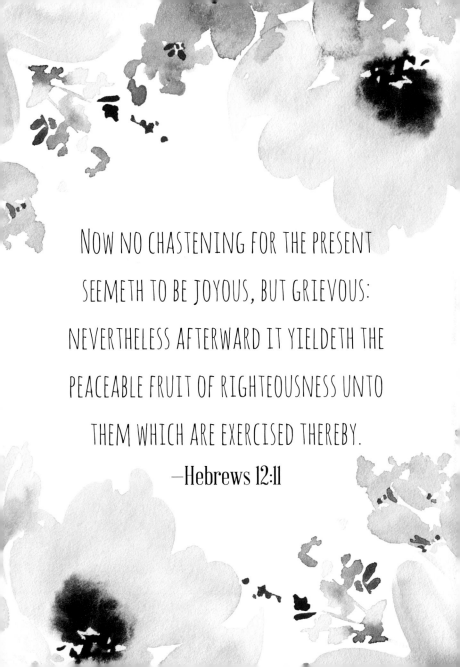

Now no chastening for the present seemeth to be joyous, but grievous: nevertheless afterward it yieldeth the peaceable fruit of righteousness unto them which are exercised thereby.

—Hebrews 12:11

Train up a child in the way he should go: and when he is old, he will not depart from it.

–Proverbs 22:6

Correct thy son, and he shall give thee rest; yea, he shall give delight unto thy soul.

—Proverbs 29:17

Arise, shine; for thy light is come, and the glory of the LORD is risen upon thee.

—Isaiah 60:1

Feed the flock of God which is among you, taking the oversight thereof, not by constraint, but willingly; not for filthy lucre, but of a ready mind; Neither as being lords over God's heritage, but being examples to the flock.

–1 Peter 5:2-3

Thine eyes did see my substance, yet being unperfect; and in thy book all my members were written, which in continuance were fashioned, when as yet there was none of them.

—Psalm 139:16

As arrows are in the hand of a mighty man;
so are children of the youth. Happy is the
man that hath his quiver full of them: they
shall not be ashamed, but they shall speak
with the enemies in the gate.

–Psalm 127:4-5

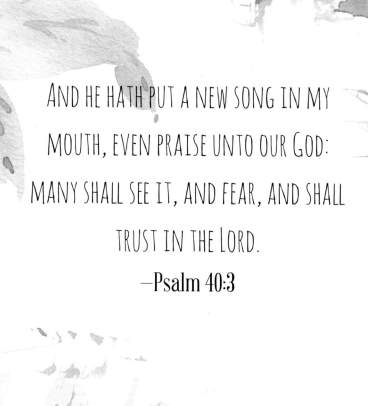

And he hath put a new song in my mouth, even praise unto our God: many shall see it, and fear, and shall trust in the Lord.

—Psalm 40:3

Therefore if any man be in Christ, he is a new creature: old things are passed away; behold, all things are become new.

−2 Corinthians 5:17

Be merciful unto me,
O Lord: for I cry
unto thee daily.

—Psalm 86:3

Trust in the LORD with all thine heart; and lean not unto thine own understanding.

–Proverbs 3:5

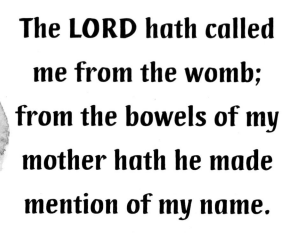

The **LORD** hath called me from the womb; from the bowels of my mother hath he made mention of my name.

–Isaiah 49:1

In all things shewing thyself
a pattern of good works: in
doctrine shewing uncorruptness,
gravity, sincerity . . .
—Titus 2:7

Now the Lord is that Spirit: and where the Spirit of the Lord is, there is liberty.

–2 Corinthians 3:17

But they that wait upon the LORD shall renew their strength; they shall mount up with wings as eagles; they shall run, and not be weary; and they shall walk, and not faint.

—Isaiah 40:31

Then they cry unto the LORD in their trouble, and he saveth them out of their distresses.

—Psalm 107:19

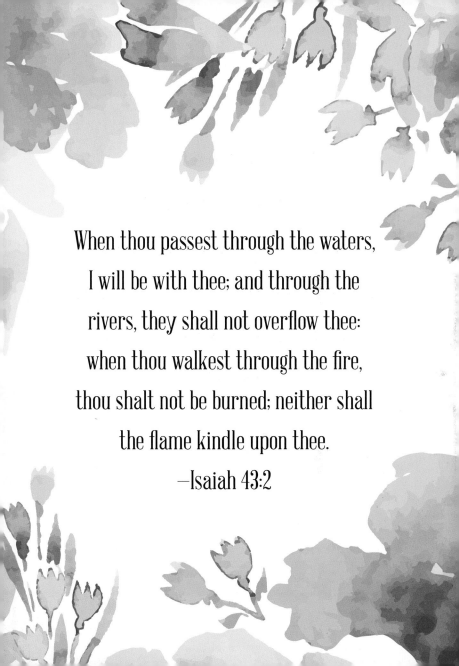

When thou passest through the waters,
I will be with thee; and through the
rivers, they shall not overflow thee:
when thou walkest through the fire,
thou shalt not be burned; neither shall
the flame kindle upon thee.

–Isaiah 43:2

Favour is deceitful, and beauty is vain: but a woman that feareth the Lord, she shall be praised.

—Proverbs 31:30

Suffer the little children
to come unto me, and forbid
them not: for of such is
the kingdom of God.

—Mark 10:14

Her children arise up, and call
her blessed; her husband also,
and he praiseth her.
—Proverbs 31:28

Have not I commanded thee? Be strong and of a good courage; be not afraid, neither be thou dismayed: for the LORD thy God is with thee whithersoever thou goest.

—Joshua 1:9

Teach me good judgment and knowledge: for I have believed thy commandments.

—Psalm 119:66

The name of the LORD is a strong tower: the righteous runneth into it, and is safe.

–Proverbs 18:10

While I live will I praise the LORD: I will sing praises unto my God while I have any being.

–Psalm 146:2

Be of good courage, and he
shall strengthen your heart,
all ye that hope in the LORD.

–Psalm 31:24

O keep my soul, and deliver me:
let me not be ashamed; for I put
my trust in thee.

—Psalm 25:20

Let the saints be joyful in glory: let them sing aloud upon their beds.

–Psalm 149:5

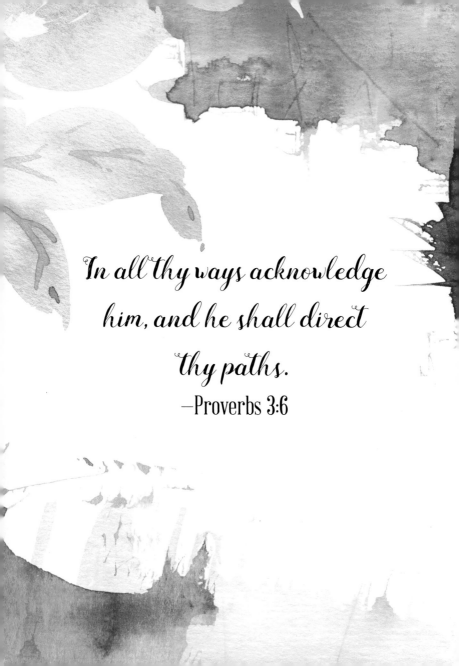

In all thy ways acknowledge him, and he shall direct thy paths.

–Proverbs 3:6

Blessed be God, even the Father
of our Lord Jesus Christ, the Father
of mercies, and the God of all comfort;
Who comforteth us in all our tribulation,
that we may be able to comfort them
which are in any trouble, by the
comfort wherewith we ourselves
are comforted of God.
–2 Corinthians 1:3-4

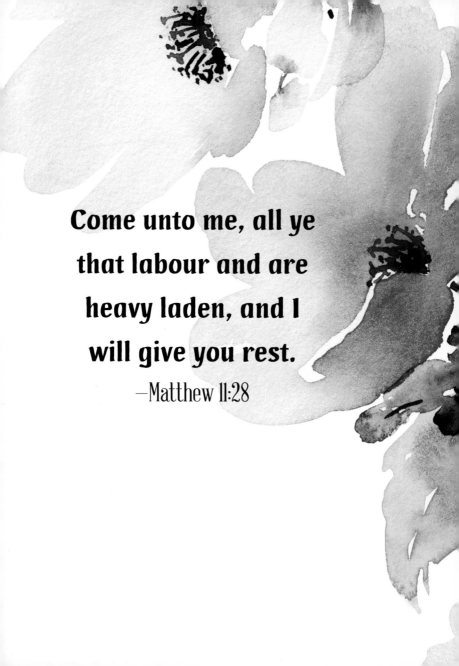

Come unto me, all ye that labour and are heavy laden, and I will give you rest.

—Matthew 11:28

Fear thou not; for I am with thee: be not dismayed; for I am thy God: I will strengthen thee; yea, I will help thee; yea, I will uphold thee with the right hand of my righteousness.

—Isaiah 41:10

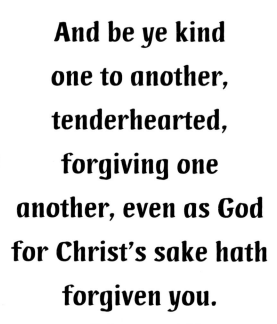

And be ye kind one to another, tenderhearted, forgiving one another, even as God for Christ's sake hath forgiven you.

–Ephesians 4:32

Peace I leave with you, my peace I give unto you: not as the world giveth, give I unto you. Let not your heart be troubled, neither let it be afraid.

—John 14:27

Restore unto me the joy of thy salvation; and uphold me with thy free spirit.

–Psalm 51:12

For I am persuaded, that neither death, nor life, nor angels, nor principalities, nor powers, nor things present, nor things to come, Nor height, nor depth, nor any other creature, shall be able to separate us from the love of God, which is in Christ Jesus our Lord.

–Romans 8:38-39

These things I have spoken unto you, that in me ye might have peace. In the world ye shall have tribulation: but be of good cheer; I have overcome the world.

—John 16:33

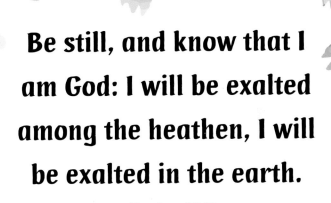

Be still, and know that I am God: I will be exalted among the heathen, I will be exalted in the earth.

–Psalm 46:10

God is our refuge and strength,
a very present help in trouble.
—Psalm 46:1

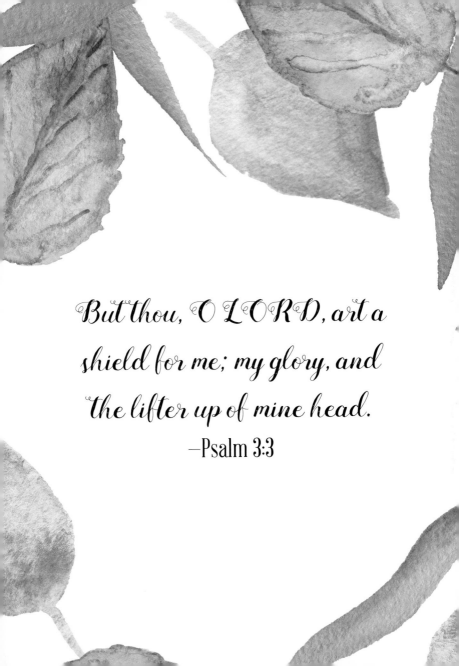

But thou, O LORD, art a shield for me; my glory, and the lifter up of mine head.

–Psalm 3:3

Therefore will not we fear,
though the earth be removed,
and though the mountains be
carried into the midst of the sea;
Though the waters thereof roar
and be troubled, though
the mountains shake with
the swelling thereof. Selah.

–Psalm 46:1-3

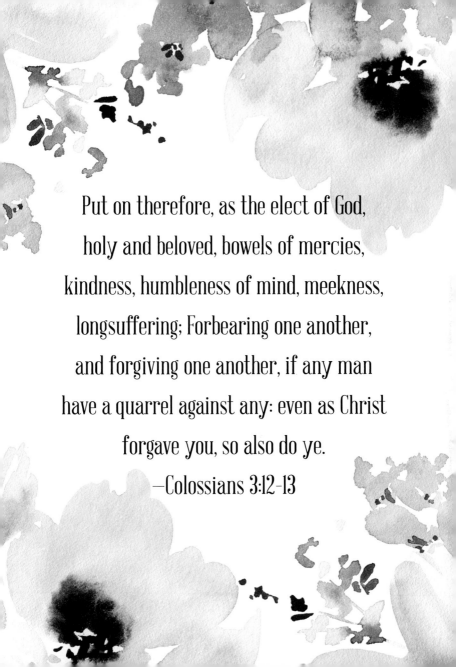

Put on therefore, as the elect of God,
holy and beloved, bowels of mercies,
kindness, humbleness of mind, meekness,
longsuffering; Forbearing one another,
and forgiving one another, if any man
have a quarrel against any: even as Christ
forgave you, so also do ye.
–Colossians 3:12-13

For God hath not given us the spirit of fear; but of power, and of love, and of a sound mind.

—2 Timothy 1:7

For he hath strengthened the bars of thy gates; he hath blessed thy children within thee.

—Psalm 147:13

I have set the LORD always before me: because he is at my right hand, I shall not be moved.

–Psalm 16:8

And he withdrew himself into the wilderness, and prayed.

—Luke 5:16

Cast thy burden upon the Lord, and he shall sustain thee: he shall never suffer the righteous to be moved.

—Psalm 55:22

The **LORD** shall increase
you more and more, you
and your children.

–Psalm 115:14

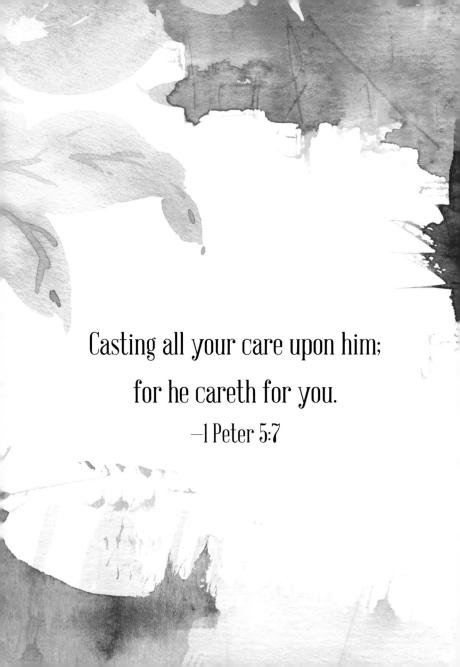

Casting all your care upon him;

for he careth for you.

—1 Peter 5:7

My soul shall be
satisfied as with
marrow and fatness;
and my mouth shall praise
thee with joyful lips . . .

—Psalm 63:5

Thou wilt keep him in perfect peace, whose mind is stayed on thee: because he trusteth in thee.

–Isaiah 26:3

For there is not a word in my tongue, but, lo, O LORD, thou knowest it altogether.

—Psalm 139:4

O give thanks unto the
LORD; for he is good:
because his mercy
endureth for ever.
—Psalm 118:1

For this child I prayed;
and the **LORD** hath given
me my petition which
I asked of him . . .

—1 Samuel 1:27

Purge me with hyssop,
and I shall be clean: wash me,
and I shall be whiter than snow.

—Psalm 51:7

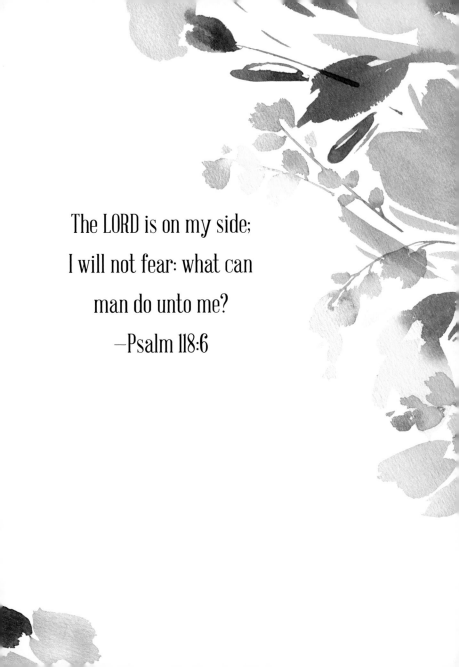

The LORD is on my side;
I will not fear: what can
man do unto me?

–Psalm 118:6

Study to shew thyself approved unto God, a workman that needeth not to be ashamed, rightly dividing the word of truth.

–2 Timothy 2:15

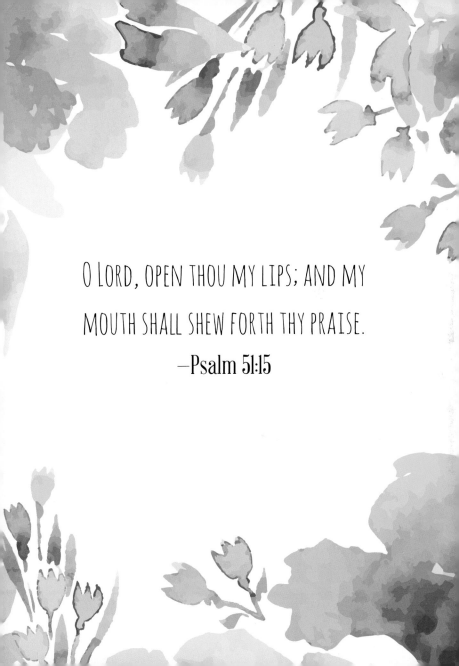

O Lord, open thou my lips; and my mouth shall shew forth thy praise.

–Psalm 51:15

It is better to trust in the
LORD than to put
confidence in man.

–Psalm 118:8

The wolf also shall dwell with the lamb, and the leopard shall lie down with the kid; and the calf and the young lion and the fatling together; and a little child shall lead them.

—Isaiah 11:6

The LORD is my strength and song,
and is become my salvation.
−Psalm 118:14

My substance was not hid from thee, when I was made in secret, and curiously wrought in the lowest parts of the earth.

—Psalm 139:15

I will praise thee: for thou hast heard me, and art become my salvation.

—Psalm 118:21

*Therefore my heart is glad,
and my glory rejoiceth: my
flesh also shall rest in hope.*

—Psalm 16:9

This is the day which the
LORD hath made; we will
rejoice and be glad in it.

—Psalm 118:24

Blessing, and glory,
and wisdom, and
thanksgiving, and honour,
and power, and might, be
unto our God for ever and
ever. Amen.

–Revelation 7:12

Thou art my God, and I will praise thee: thou art my God, I will exalt thee.

—Psalm 118:28

Out of the mouth of babes and sucklings hast thou ordained strength because of thine enemies, that thou mightest still the enemy and the avenger.

–Psalm 8:2

As one whom his mother
comforteth, so will I
comfort you . . .

—Isaiah 66:13

Let Israel hope in the LORD:
for with the LORD there is
mercy, and with him is
plenteous redemption.

—Psalm 130:7

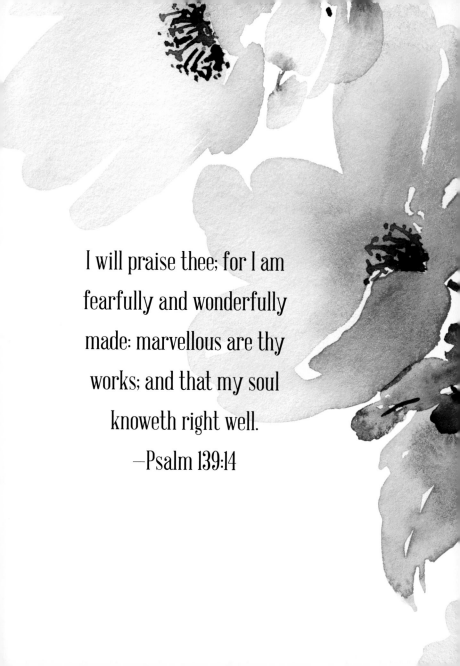

I will praise thee; for I am
fearfully and wonderfully
made: marvellous are thy
works; and that my soul
knoweth right well.

—Psalm 139:14

For his anger endureth but a moment; in his favour is life: weeping may endure for a night, but joy cometh in the morning.

—Psalm 30:5

And we know that all things
work together for good to
them that love God, to them
who are the called according
to his purpose.

—Romans 8:28

And when it was day, he departed and went into a desert place . . .

–Luke 4:42

And now abideth faith, hope, charity, these three; but the greatest of these is charity.

–1 Corinthians 13:13

O turn unto me, and have mercy upon me; give thy strength unto thy servant, and save the son of thine handmaid.

—Psalm 86:16

Do all things without murmurings and disputings: That ye may be blameless and harmless, the sons of God, without rebuke, in the midst of a crooked and perverse nation, among whom ye shine as lights in the world . . .

–Philippians 2:14-15

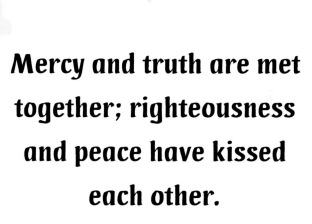

Mercy and truth are met
together; righteousness
and peace have kissed
each other.

—Psalm 85:10

Finally, brethren, whatsoever things
are true, whatsoever things are honest,
whatsoever things are just, whatsoever
things are pure, whatsoever things are
lovely, whatsoever things are of good
report; if there be any virtue, and if there
be any praise, think on these things.

–Philippians 4:8

Preserve me,
O God: for in thee
do I put my trust.

—Psalm 16:1

And Mary said, My soul doth magnify the Lord, And my spirit hath rejoiced in God my Saviour. For he hath regarded the low estate of his handmaiden: for, behold, from henceforth all generations shall call me blessed. For he that is mighty hath done to me great things; and holy is his name. And his mercy is on them that fear him from generation to generation.

–Luke 1:46-50

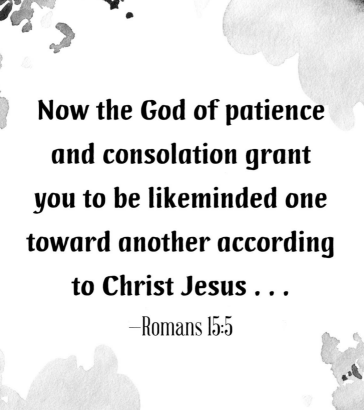

Now the God of patience
and consolation grant
you to be likeminded one
toward another according
to Christ Jesus . . .

–Romans 15:5

**And God did rest
the seventh day
from all his works.**

–Hebrews 4:4

Thou wilt shew me the path of life: in thy presence is fulness of joy; at thy right hand there are pleasures for evermore.

—Psalm 16:11

I can do all things
through Christ which
strengtheneth me.

–Philippians 4:13

Give ear to my words,
O LORD, consider my
meditation.

–Psalm 5:1

And ye shall seek me, and find me, when ye shall search for me with all your heart.

—Jeremiah 29:13

[Love] doth not behave itself
unseemly, seeketh not her
own, is not easily provoked,
thinketh no evil . . .

–1 Corinthians 13:5

Surely goodness and mercy shall follow me all the days of my life: and I will dwell in the house of the **LORD** for ever.

—Psalm 23:6

Let my prayer come before thee: incline thine ear unto my cry . . .

—Psalm 88:2

Trust in him at all times; ye people,
pour out your heart before him:
God is a refuge for us. Selah.

–Psalm 62:8

For we are his
workmanship,
created in Christ
Jesus unto good
works, which God
hath before ordained
that we should walk
in them.

–Ephesians 2:10

Fear not: for I have redeemed thee, I have called thee by thy name; thou art mine.

–Isaiah 43:1b

I will both lay me down
in peace, and sleep: for
thou, Lord, only makest
me dwell in safety.

–Psalm 4:8

Enlarge the place of thy tent,
and let them stretch forth the
curtains of thine habitations:
spare not, lengthen thy cords, and
strengthen thy stakes . . .

–Isaiah 54:2

For I will set mine eyes upon them for good, and I will bring them again to this land: and I will build them, and not pull them down; and I will plant them, and not pluck them up.

–Jeremiah 24:6

Commit thy works unto the LORD, and thy thoughts shall be established.

–Proverbs 16:3

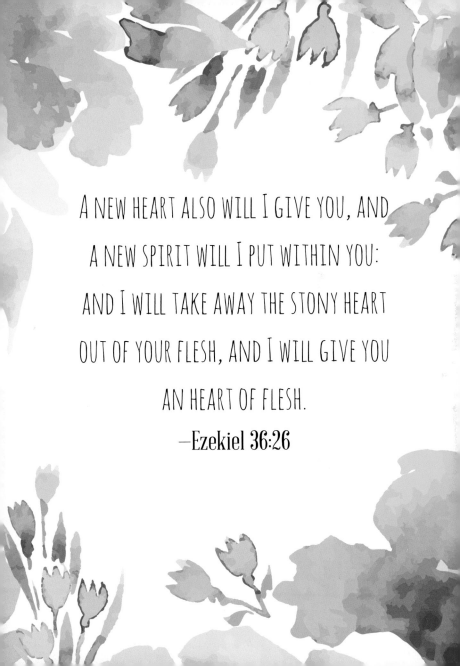

A new heart also will I give you, and a new spirit will I put within you: and I will take away the stony heart out of your flesh, and I will give you an heart of flesh.

—Ezekiel 36:26

Behold, how good and how pleasant it is for brethren to dwell together in unity!

—Psalm 133:1

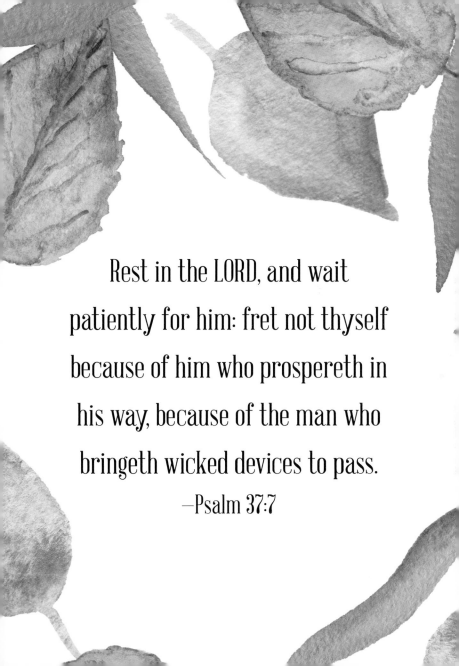

Rest in the LORD, and wait patiently for him: fret not thyself because of him who prospereth in his way, because of the man who bringeth wicked devices to pass.

–Psalm 37:7

And why take ye thought for raiment? Consider the lilies of the field, how they grow; they toil not, neither do they spin: And yet I say unto you, That even Solomon in all his glory was not arrayed like one of these.

—Matthew 6:28-29

Wait on the LORD, and keep his way

–Psalm 37:34a

He shall feed his flock like a shepherd: he shall gather the lambs with his arm, and carry them in his bosom, and shall gently lead those that are with young.

—Isaiah 40:11

The LORD lift up his countenance upon thee, and give thee peace.

–Numbers 6:26

And Jesus answered and said unto her, Martha, Martha, thou art careful and troubled about many things: But one thing is needful: and Mary hath chosen that good part, which shall not be taken away from her.

—Luke 10:41-42

In God is my
salvation and my
glory: the rock of
my strength, and my
refuge, is in God.

–Psalm 62:7

I will bless the LORD, who hath given me counsel: my reins also instruct me in the night seasons.

—Psalm 16:7

And all thy children shall
be taught of the LORD;
and great shall be the peace
of thy children.

—Isaiah 54:13

Return unto thy rest, O my
soul; for the LORD hath dealt
bountifully with thee.

–Psalm 116:7

But rather seek ye the kingdom of God; and all these things shall be added unto you.

—Luke 12:31

Thou art all fair, my love; there
is no spot in thee.

–Song of Solomon 4:7

He shall deliver thee in six troubles: yea, in seven there shall no evil touch thee.

—Job 5:19

O LORD my God, in thee do I put my trust: save me from all them that persecute me, and deliver me . . .

–Psalm 7:1

She girdeth her loins with strength, and strengtheneth her arms.

—Proverbs 31:17

In the day when I cried thou
answeredst me, and strengthenedst
me with strength in my soul.
—Psalm 138:3

Now unto him that is able to do exceeding abundantly above all that we ask or think, according to the power that worketh in us . . .

–Ephesians 3:20

I will worship toward thy holy temple, and praise thy name for thy lovingkindness and for thy truth: for thou hast magnified thy word above all thy name.

–Psalm 138:2

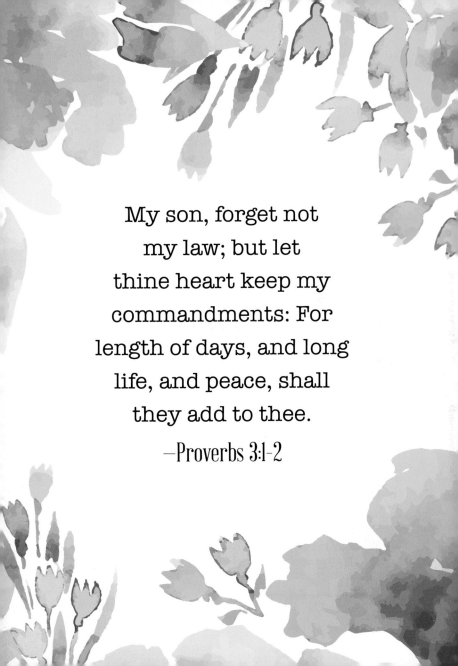

My son, forget not
my law; but let
thine heart keep my
commandments: For
length of days, and long
life, and peace, shall
they add to thee.

—Proverbs 3:1-2

There is therefore now no condemnation to them which are in Christ Jesus, who walk not after the flesh, but after the Spirit.

–Romans 8:1

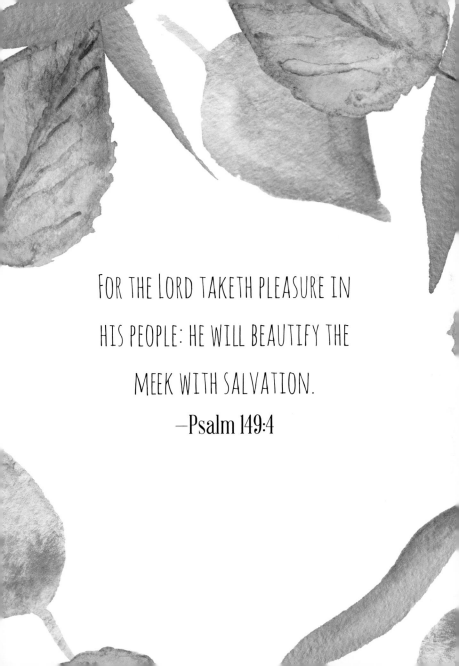

For the Lord taketh pleasure in his people: he will beautify the meek with salvation.

—Psalm 149:4

But the God of all grace, who hath called us unto his eternal glory by Christ Jesus, after that ye have suffered a while, make you perfect, stablish, strengthen, settle you.

–1 Peter 5:10

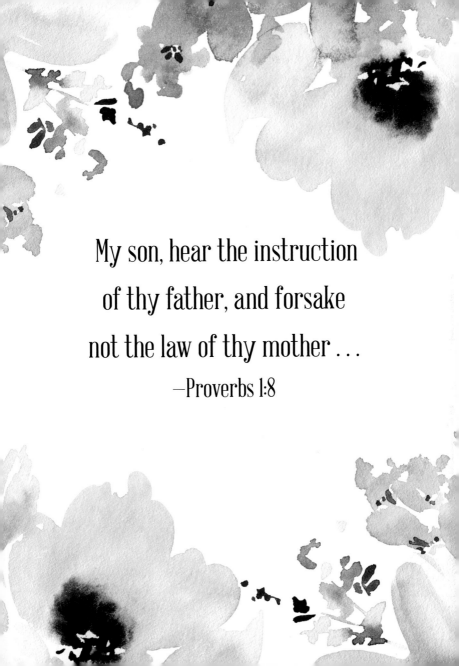

My son, hear the instruction
of thy father, and forsake
not the law of thy mother . . .

–Proverbs 1:8

The young lions do lack, and suffer hunger: but they that seek the LORD shall not want any good thing.

—Psalm 34:10

The Lord is nigh unto them that are of a broken heart; and saveth such as be of a contrite spirit.

–Psalm 34:18

The LORD redeemeth the soul of his servants: and none of them that trust in him shall be desolate.

–Psalm 34:22

. . . the joy of the **LORD** is your strength.

–Nehemiah 8:10

. . . for your heavenly Father knoweth that ye have need of all these things. But seek ye first the kingdom of God, and his righteousness; and all these things shall be added unto you.

—Matthew 6:32-33

And he shall turn the heart of the fathers
to the children, and the heart of the
children to their fathers . . .

—Malachi 4:6

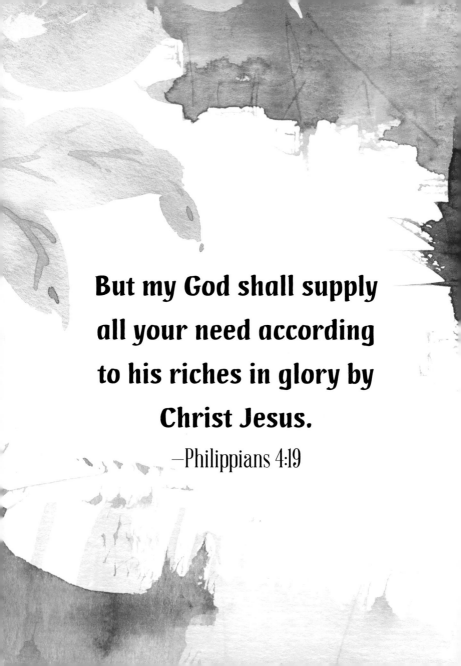

But my God shall supply all your need according to his riches in glory by Christ Jesus.

–Philippians 4:19

Wherefore, my beloved brethren, let every man be swift to hear, slow to speak, slow to wrath . . .

—James 1:19

. . . your Father knoweth
what things ye have need
of, before ye ask him.
–Matthew 6:8b

**Shew me thy ways,
O LORD; teach me
thy paths.**

–Psalm 25:4

He that spared
not his own Son,
but delivered him
up for us all, how
shall he not with
him also freely give
us all things?
—Romans 8:32

. . . for I have learned, in whatsoever state I am, therewith to be content.

—Philippians 4:11

And even to your old age
I am he; and even to hoar
hairs will I carry you: I
have made, and I will bear;
even I will carry, and will
deliver you.

–Isaiah 46:4

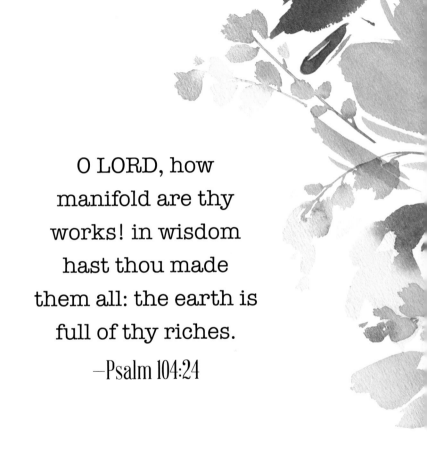

O LORD, how manifold are thy works! in wisdom hast thou made them all: the earth is full of thy riches.

—Psalm 104:24

Hearken, my beloved brethren, Hath not God chosen the poor of this world rich in faith, and heirs of the kingdom which he hath promised to them that love him?

–James 2:5

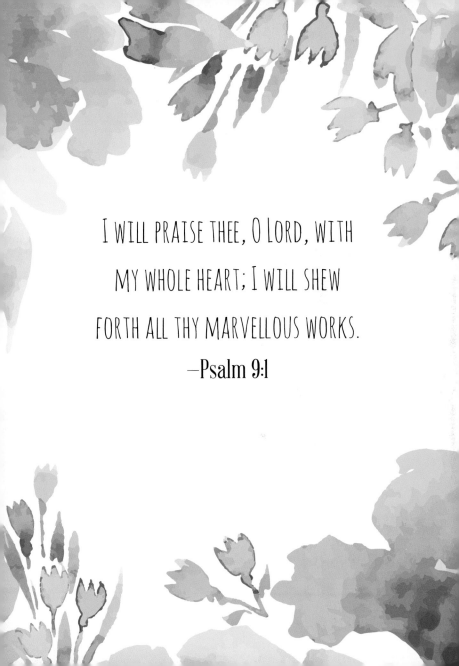

I will praise thee, O Lord, with my whole heart; I will shew forth all thy marvellous works.

–Psalm 9:1

The LORD knoweth the days of the upright: and their inheritance shall be for ever.

–Psalm 37:18

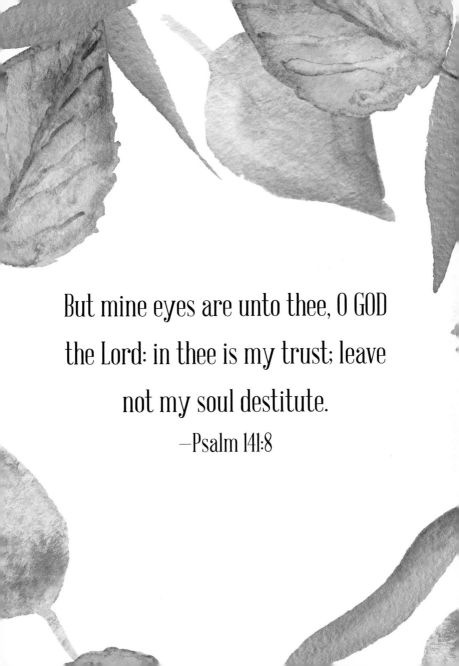

But mine eyes are unto thee, O GOD
the Lord: in thee is my trust; leave
not my soul destitute.

—Psalm 141:8

Let us therefore come boldly unto the throne of grace, that we may obtain mercy, and find grace to help in time of need.

—Hebrews 4:16

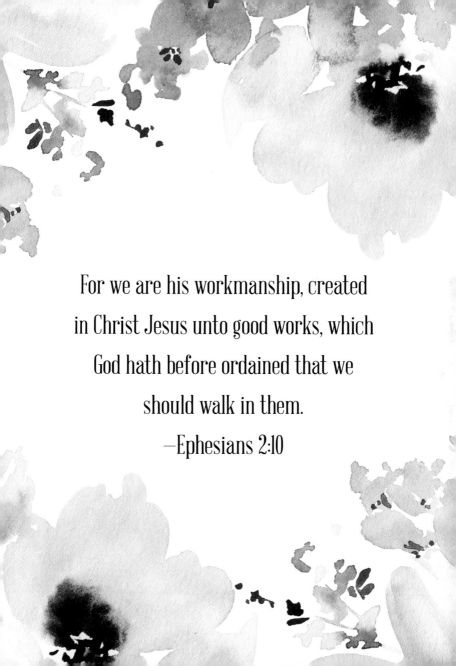

For we are his workmanship, created in Christ Jesus unto good works, which God hath before ordained that we should walk in them.

—Ephesians 2:10

Peace, peace to him that is far off, and to him that is near, saith the Lord; and I will heal him.

—Isaiah 57:19

And therefore will the LORD wait, that he may be gracious unto you, and therefore will he be exalted, that he may have mercy upon you: for the LORD is a God of judgment: blessed are all they that wait for him.

—Isaiah 30:18

Let every thing that hath breath praise the LORD. Praise ye the LORD.

–Psalm 150:6

Thou art worthy, O Lord, to receive glory
and honour and power: for thou hast
created all things, and for thy pleasure
they are and were created.

—Revelations 4:11

For I have satiated the weary soul, and I have replenished every sorrowful soul.

—Jeremiah 31:25

Every good gift and every perfect gift
is from above, and cometh down from
the Father of lights, with whom is no
variableness, neither shadow of turning.

—James 1:17

Blessed are they that
mourn: for they shall
be comforted.

—Matthew 5:4

To do justice and judgment is more acceptable to the Lord than sacrifice.

—Proverbs 21:3

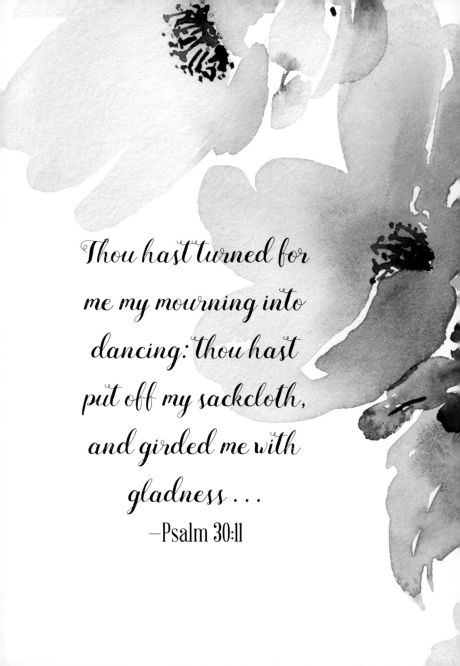

Thou hast turned for me my mourning into dancing: thou hast put off my sackcloth, and girded me with gladness . . .

—Psalm 30:11

Thou openest thine hand,
and satisfiest the desire
of every living thing.
—Psalm 145:16

My voice shalt thou hear
in the morning, O Lord;
in the morning will I
direct my prayer unto
thee, and will look up.

–Psalm 5:3

For he satisfieth the longing soul, and filleth the hungry soul with goodness.

–Psalm 107:9

Keep thy heart with all diligence; for out of it are the issues of life.

—Proverbs 4:23

Stand fast therefore in
the liberty wherewith
Christ hath made
us free, and be not
entangled again with
the yoke of bondage.

–Galatians 5:1

For he shall give his angels charge over thee, to keep thee in all thy ways.

—Psalm 91:11

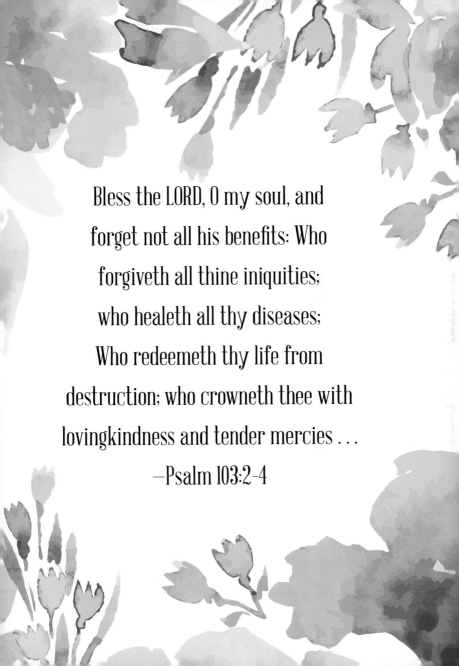

Bless the LORD, O my soul, and forget not all his benefits: Who forgiveth all thine iniquities; who healeth all thy diseases; Who redeemeth thy life from destruction; who crowneth thee with lovingkindness and tender mercies . . .

–Psalm 103:2-4

My soul waiteth for the Lord more than they that watch for the morning: I say, more than they that watch for the morning.

—Psalm 130:6

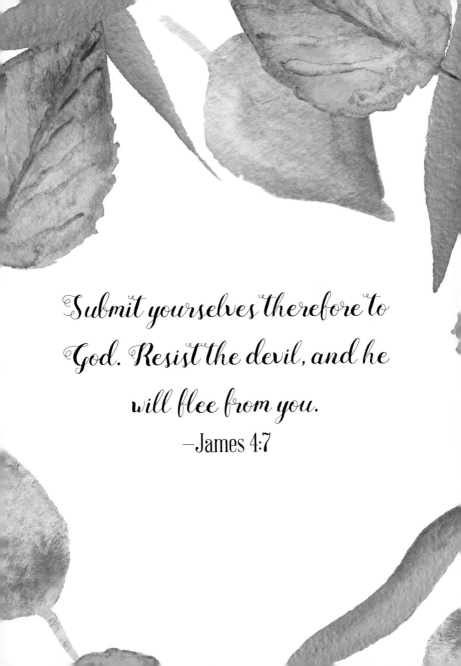

Submit yourselves therefore to God. Resist the devil, and he will flee from you.

–James 4:7

Mine eyes are ever toward
the LORD; for he shall pluck
my feet out of the net.

—Psalm 25:15

The **LORD** is my shepherd;
I shall not want.

—Psalm 23:1

Draw nigh to God, and he will draw nigh to you. Cleanse your hands, ye sinners; and purify your hearts, ye double minded.

—James 4:8

My help cometh from the LORD, which made heaven and earth.

—Psalm 121:2

For in that he himself hath
suffered being tempted,
he is able to succour them
that are tempted.

—Hebrews 2:18

O satisfy us early with thy mercy; that we may rejoice and be glad all our days.

–Psalm 90:14

Behold, happy is the man whom God correcteth: therefore despise not thou the chastening of the Almighty.

—Job 5:17

. . . for he that loveth another
hath fulfilled the law.

–Romans 13:8b

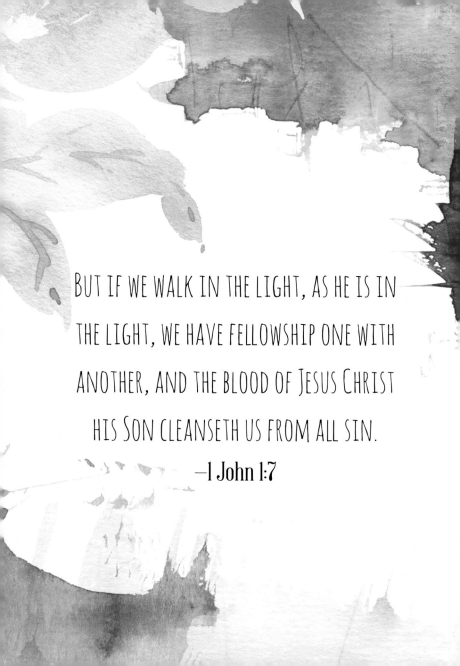

But if we walk in the light, as he is in the light, we have fellowship one with another, and the blood of Jesus Christ his Son cleanseth us from all sin.

–1 John 1:7

Deliver me out of the mire, and let me not sink: let me be delivered from them that hate me, and out of the deep waters.

—Psalm 69:14

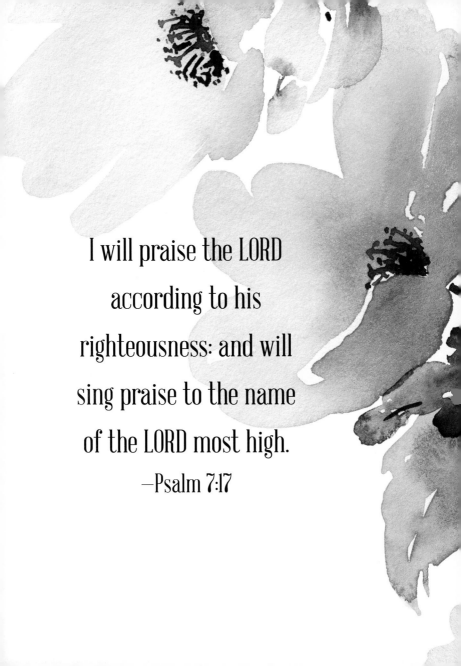

I will praise the LORD
according to his
righteousness: and will
sing praise to the name
of the LORD most high.

–Psalm 7:17

And the **LORD** shall help them, and deliver them: he shall deliver them from the wicked, and save them, because they trust in him.

–Psalm 37:40

Whatsoever thy hand
findeth to do, do it with
thy might . . .
—Ecclesiastes 9:10a

He only is my rock and my salvation:
he is my defence; I shall not be moved.

—Psalm 62:6

Like as a father pitieth his children, so the LORD pitieth them that fear him.

—Psalm 103:13

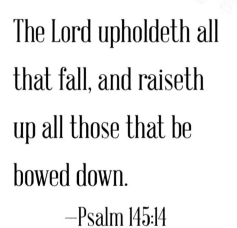

The Lord upholdeth all
that fall, and raiseth
up all those that be
bowed down.

—Psalm 145:14

(For the LORD thy God is a merciful God;) he will not forsake thee, neither destroy thee, nor forget the covenant of thy fathers which he sware unto them.

—Deuteronomy 4:31

O clap your hands, all ye people; shout unto God with the voice of triumph.

—Psalm 47:1

And the Lord shall guide thee continually, and satisfy thy soul in drought, and make fat thy bones: and thou shalt be like a watered garden, and like a spring of water, whose waters fail not.

—Isaiah 58:11

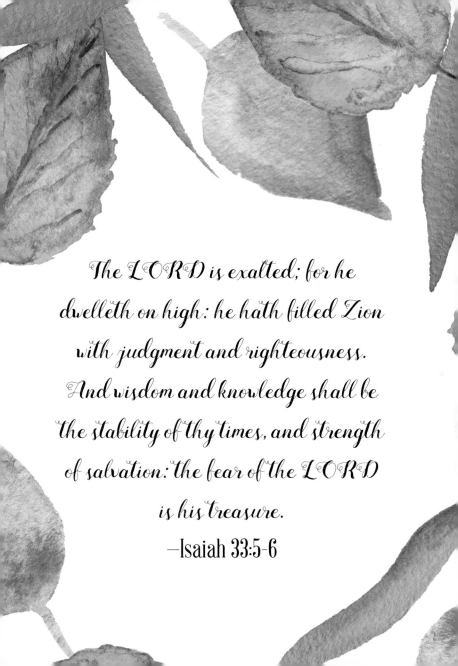

The LORD is exalted; for he dwelleth on high: he hath filled Zion with judgment and righteousness. And wisdom and knowledge shall be the stability of thy times, and strength of salvation: the fear of the LORD is his treasure.

–Isaiah 33:5-6

Who is a God like unto thee, that pardoneth iniquity, and passeth by the transgression of the remnant of his heritage? he retaineth not his anger for ever, because he delighteth in mercy.

—Micah 7:18

Verily I say unto you,
Except ye be converted,
and become as little
children, ye shall not
enter into the kingdom of
heaven.

–Matthew 18:3

And Jesus saith unto them, Yea; have ye never read, Out of the mouth of babes and sucklings thou hast perfected praise?

—Matthew 21:16

Teach me to do thy will;
for thou art my God: thy
spirit is good; lead me into
the land of uprightness.

–Psalm 143:10

And every man that hath this hope in him purifieth himself, even as he is pure.

—1 John 3:3

Hear me when I call, O God of my righteousness: thou hast enlarged me when I was in distress; have mercy upon me, and hear my prayer.

—Psalm 4:1

Make thy face to shine
upon thy servant: save me
for thy mercies' sake.

—Psalm 31:16

Take my yoke upon you, and
learn of me; for I am meek and
lowly in heart: and ye shall
find rest unto your souls.

—Matthew 11:29

As far as the east is from the west, so far hath he removed our transgressions from us.

—Psalm 103:12

And whatsoever ye do in word or deed, do all in the name of the Lord Jesus, giving thanks to God and the Father by him.

—Colossians 3:17

The LORD is thy keeper: the LORD is thy shade upon thy right hand.

–Psalm 121:5

A man's heart deviseth
his way: but the LORD
directeth his steps.

–Proverbs 16:9

I HAVE BLOTTED OUT,
AS A THICK CLOUD, THY
TRANSGRESSIONS, AND, AS
A CLOUD, THY SINS: RETURN
UNTO ME; FOR I HAVE
REDEEMED THEE.
—Isaiah 44:22

For I am the LORD,

I change not . . .

–Malachi 3:6a

The LORD shall preserve thy going out and thy coming in from this time forth, and even for evermore.

—Psalm 121:8

For ye shall go out with joy, and be led forth with peace: the mountains and the hills shall break forth before you into singing, and all the trees of the field shall clap their hands.

—Isaiah 55:12

For thou art an holy people unto the Lord thy God: the Lord thy God hath chosen thee to be a special people unto himself, above all people that are upon the face of the earth.

—Deuteronomy 7:6

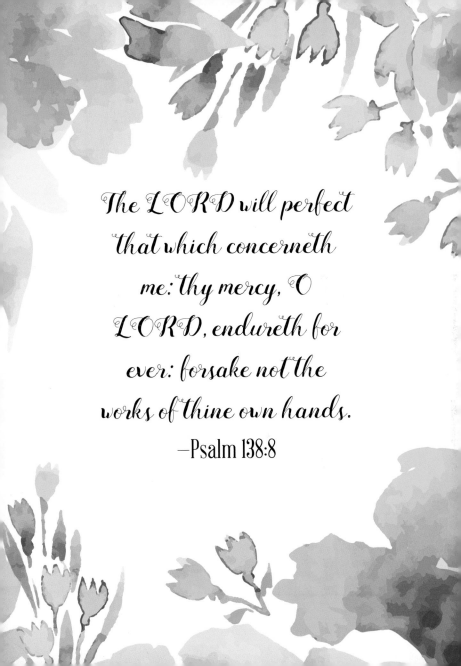

The LORD will perfect
that which concerneth
me: thy mercy, O
LORD, endureth for
ever: forsake not the
works of thine own hands.

–Psalm 138:8

For I acknowledge my transgressions: and my sin is ever before me.

–Psalm 51:3

Justice and judgment are the habitation of thy throne: mercy and truth shall go before thy face.

—Psalm 89:14

Behold, the LORD God will help me; who is he that shall condemn me? lo, they all shall wax old as a garment; the moth shall eat them up.

—Isaiah 50:9

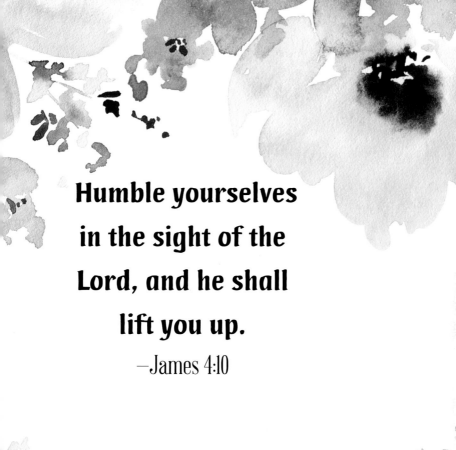

Humble yourselves in the sight of the Lord, and he shall lift you up.

–James 4:10

As thou knowest not what is the way of the spirit, nor how the bones do grow in the womb of her that is with child: even so thou knowest not the works of God who maketh all.

—Ecclesiastes 11:5

Beloved, now are we the sons of God, and it doth not yet appear what we shall be: but we know that, when he shall appear, we shall be like him; for we shall see him as he is.

–1 John 3:2

My son, give me thine heart, and let thine eyes observe my ways.

–Proverbs 23:26

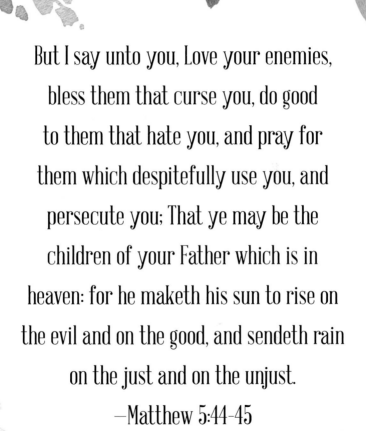

But I say unto you, Love your enemies,
bless them that curse you, do good
to them that hate you, and pray for
them which despitefully use you, and
persecute you; That ye may be the
children of your Father which is in
heaven: for he maketh his sun to rise on
the evil and on the good, and sendeth rain
on the just and on the unjust.

–Matthew 5:44-45

[Love] beareth all things, believeth all things, hopeth all things, endureth all things.

—1 Corinthians 13:7

And if children, then heirs; heirs of God,
and joint-heirs with Christ; if so be that
we suffer with him, that we may be also
glorified together.

–Romans 8:17

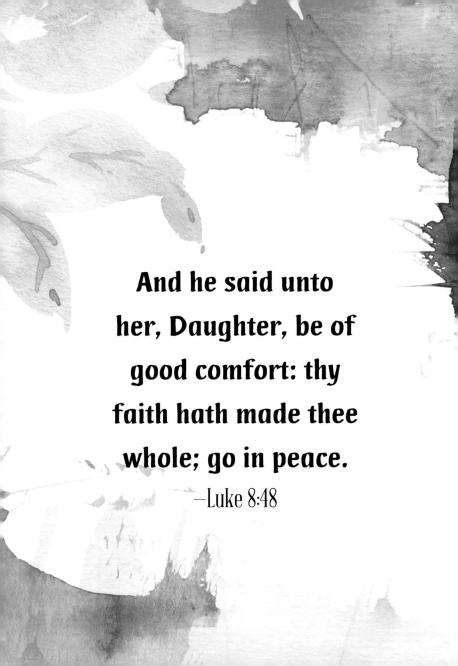

And he said unto her, Daughter, be of good comfort: thy faith hath made thee whole; go in peace.

–Luke 8:48

The Spirit itself beareth
witness with our spirit, that
we are the children of God . . .

—Romans 8:16

Create in me a
clean heart, O
God; and renew
a right spirit
within me.

–Psalm 51:10

For ye have not received the spirit of bondage again to fear; but ye have received the Spirit of adoption, whereby we cry, Abba, Father.

—Romans 8:15

And be not conformed
to this world: but be
ye transformed by the
renewing of your mind,
that ye may prove what is
that good, and acceptable,
and perfect, will of God.

—Romans 12:2

And above all these things put on charity, which is the bond of perfectness.

–Colossians 3:14

HEARKEN UNTO THE VOICE OF MY
CRY, MY KING, AND MY GOD: FOR
UNTO THEE WILL I PRAY.
—Psalm 5:2

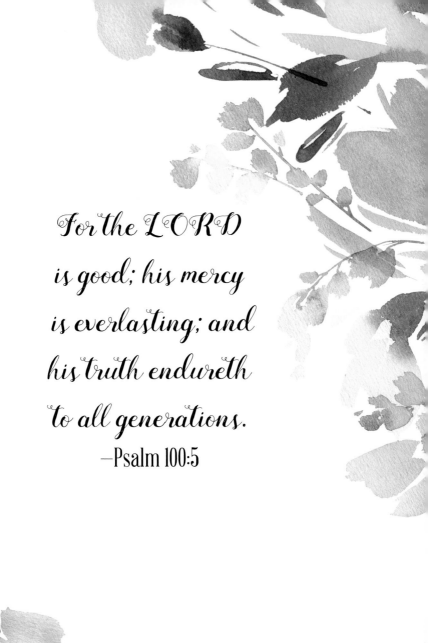

For the LORD
is good; his mercy
is everlasting; and
his truth endureth
to all generations.
–Psalm 100:5

Turn thou us unto thee, **O LORD**, and we shall be turned; renew our days as of old.

–Lamentations 5:21

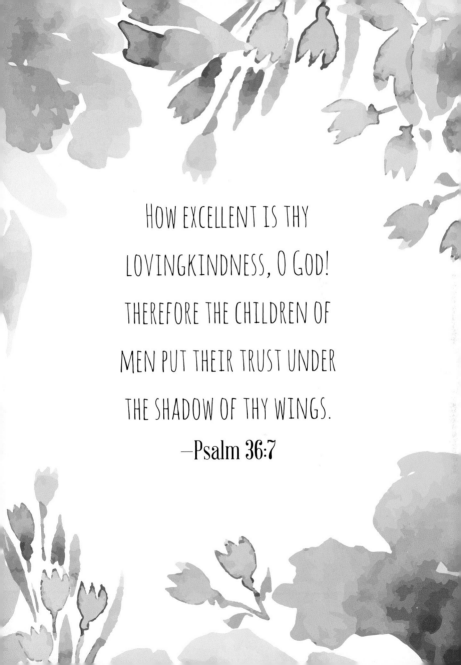

How excellent is thy lovingkindness, O God! therefore the children of men put their trust under the shadow of thy wings.

—Psalm 36:7

For thou, LORD, wilt bless the righteous; with favour wilt thou compass him as with a shield.

–Psalm 5:12

The **LORD** hath appeared of old unto me, saying, Yea, I have loved thee with an everlasting love: therefore with lovingkindness have I drawn thee.

–Jeremiah 31:3

I will abide in thy
tabernacle for ever: I will
trust in the covert of thy
wings. Selah.

—Psalm 61:4

And hope maketh not
ashamed; because the
love of God is shed
abroad in our hearts
by the Holy Ghost
which is given unto us.

–Romans 5:5

As in water face answereth to face, so the heart of man to man.

—Proverbs 27:19

That Christ may dwell in your hearts by faith; that ye, being rooted and grounded in love, May be able to comprehend with all saints what is the breadth, and length, and depth, and height; And to know the love of Christ, which passeth knowledge, that ye might be filled with all the fulness of God.

–Ephesians 3:17-19

My times are in thy hand:
deliver me from the hand of
mine enemies, and from them
that persecute me.

—Psalm 31:15

Thy mercy, **O LORD**, is in the heavens; and thy faithfulness reacheth unto the clouds.

—Psalm 36:5

... the smell of my son is
as the smell of a field which
the LORD hath blessed ...

—Genesis 27:27

For whom the LORD loveth
he correcteth; even as a father
the son in whom he delighteth.

–Proverbs 3:12

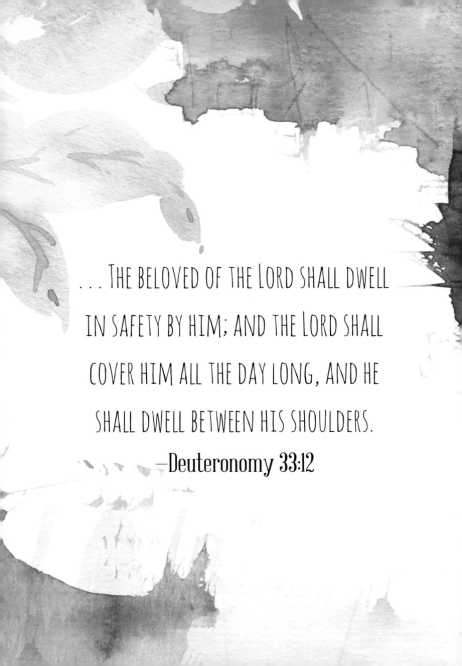

. . . The beloved of the Lord shall dwell in safety by him; and the Lord shall cover him all the day long, and he shall dwell between his shoulders.

—Deuteronomy 33:12

For the mountains shall depart, and the hills be removed; but my kindness shall not depart from thee, neither shall the covenant of my peace be removed, saith the LORD that hath mercy on thee.

–Isaiah 54:10

Say not thou, What is the cause that the former days were better than these? for thou dost not enquire wisely concerning this.

—Ecclesiastes 7:10

Since thou wast precious
in my sight, thou hast been
honourable, and I have
loved thee: therefore will
I give men for thee, and
people for thy life.

–Isaiah 43:4

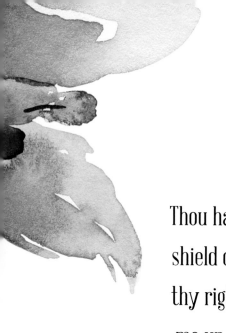

Thou hast also given me the shield of thy salvation: and thy right hand hath holden me up, and thy gentleness hath made me great.

—Psalm 18:35

The eyes of the
LORD are upon the
righteous, and his
ears are open unto
their cry.

—Psalm 34:15

There be many that say, Who will shew us any good? Lord, lift thou up the light of thy countenance upon us.

—Psalm 4:6

And the peace of
God, which passeth
all understanding,
shall keep your
hearts and minds
through Christ
Jesus.

–Philippians 4:7

My flesh and my heart faileth: but
God is the strength of my heart,
and my portion for ever.

—Psalm 73:26

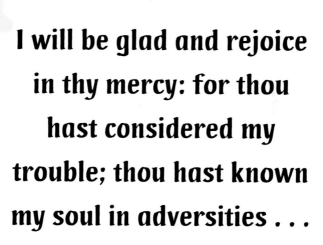

I will be glad and rejoice in thy mercy: for thou hast considered my trouble; thou hast known my soul in adversities . . .

—Psalm 31:7

The earth is the Lord's, and the fulness thereof; the world, and they that dwell therein.

—Psalm 24:1

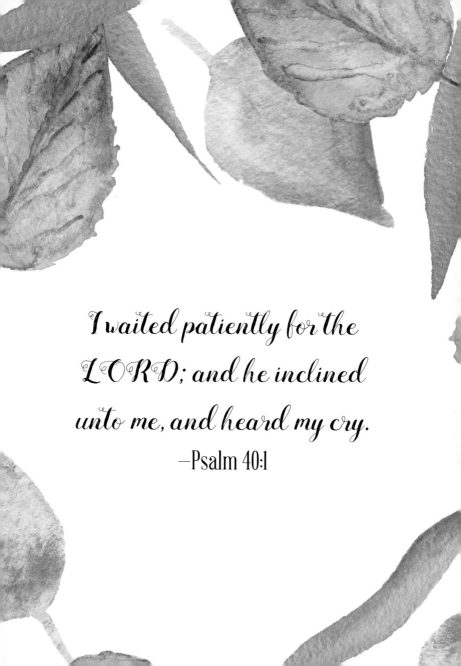

I waited patiently for the
LORD; and he inclined
unto me, and heard my cry.

—Psalm 40:1

Thou hast heard my voice: hide not thine ear at my breathing, at my cry.

–Lamentations 3:56

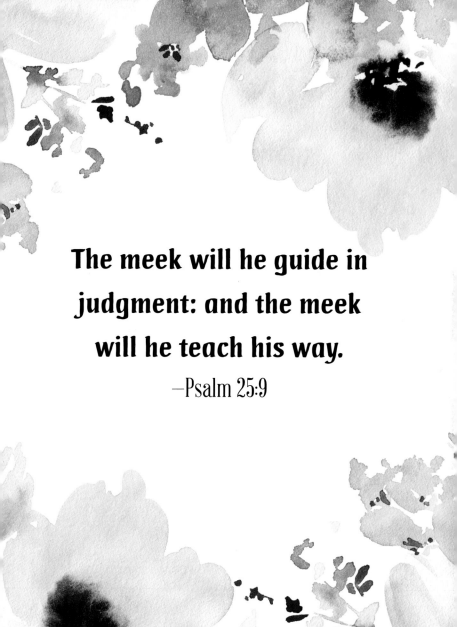

The meek will he guide in judgment: and the meek will he teach his way.

–Psalm 25:9

Thou knowest my downsitting and mine uprising, thou understandest my thought afar off.

—Psalm 139:2

I will be glad and rejoice in thee: I will sing praise to thy name, O thou most High.

–Psalm 9:2

If we believe not, yet he abideth faithful: he cannot deny himself.

—2 Timothy 2:13

**Better is a dry
morsel, and quietness
therewith, than an
house full of sacrifices
with strife.**

–Proverbs 17:1

Thou compassest my path and my lying down, and art acquainted with all my ways.

—Psalm 139:3

**O LORD my God, I
cried unto thee, and
thou hast healed me.**

–Psalm 30:2

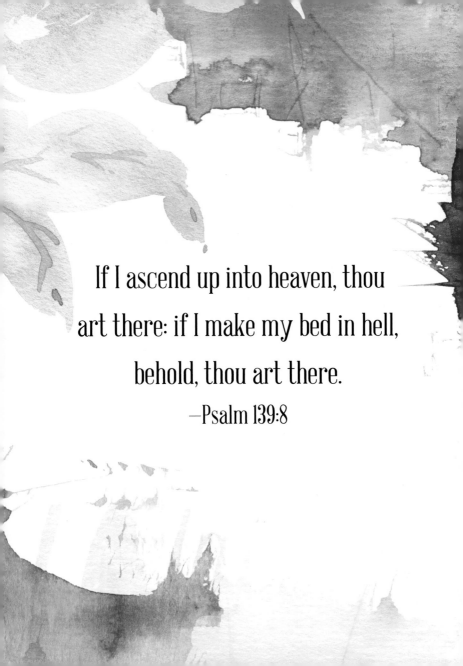

If I ascend up into heaven, thou
art there: if I make my bed in hell,
behold, thou art there.

—Psalm 139:8

One thing have I desired of the LORD, that will I seek after; that I may dwell in the house of the LORD all the days of my life, to behold the beauty of the LORD, and to enquire in his temple.

–Psalm 27:4

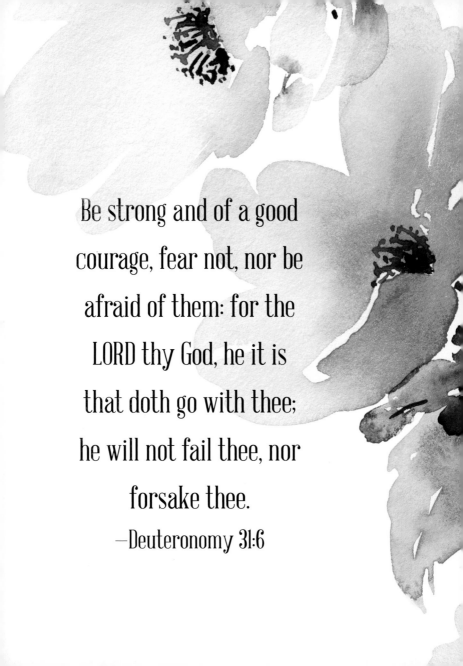

Be strong and of a good courage, fear not, nor be afraid of them: for the LORD thy God, he it is that doth go with thee; he will not fail thee, nor forsake thee.

–Deuteronomy 31:6

The **LORD** will give strength unto his people; the **LORD** will bless his people with peace.

—Psalm 29:11

The grace of our Lord Jesus Christ be with you all. Amen.

–Philippians 4:23

Have mercy upon me, O God, according to thy lovingkindness: according unto the multitude of thy tender mercies blot out my transgressions.

–Psalm 51:1

Let the heaven and earth praise him, the seas, and every thing that moveth therein.

—Psalm 69:34

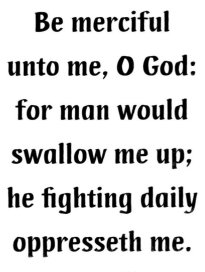

**Be merciful
unto me, O God:
for man would
swallow me up;
he fighting daily
oppresseth me.**

–Psalm 56:1

Great is our Lord, and of great power:

his understanding is infinite.

—Psalm 147:5

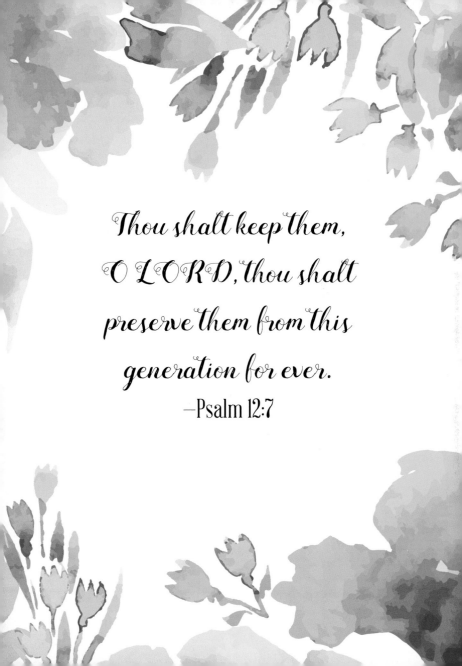

Thou shalt keep them,
O LORD, thou shalt
preserve them from this
generation for ever.
—Psalm 12:7

Call unto me, and I will
answer thee, and show thee
great and mighty things,
which thou knowest not.
—Jeremiah 33:3

Be not far from me; for trouble is near; for there is none to help.

—Psalm 22:11

If ye then, being evil, know how to give good gifts unto your children, how much more shall your Father which is in heaven give good things to them that ask him?

—Matthew 7:11

Keep me as the apple of
the eye, hide me under the
shadow of thy wings . . .
—Psalm 17:8

He only is my rock and my salvation; he is my defence; I shall not be greatly moved.

–Psalm 62:2

Ask, and it shall be given you; seek, and ye shall find; knock, and it shall be opened unto you . . .

—Matthew 7:7

And I will bring the blind by a way that they knew not; I will lead them in paths that they have not known: I will make darkness light before them, and crooked things straight. These things will I do unto them, and not forsake them.

–Isaiah 42:16

Let not the waterflood
overflow me, neither let
the deep swallow me up,
and let not the pit shut
her mouth upon me.

–Psalm 69:15

Then shall ye call upon me, and ye shall go and pray unto me, and I will hearken unto you.

—Jeremiah 29:12

Likewise the Spirit also helpeth our
infirmities: for we know not what we
should pray for as we ought: but the
Spirit itself maketh intercession for us
with groanings which cannot be uttered.

–Romans 8:26

And this is the confidence that we have in him, that, if we ask any thing according to his will, he heareth us . . .

—1 John 5:14

Remember not the sins of my youth, nor my transgressions: according to thy mercy remember thou me for thy goodness' sake, O Lord.

–Psalm 25:7

The lines are fallen unto me in pleasant places; yea, I have a goodly heritage.

–Psalm 16:6

He will not suffer thy foot to be moved: he that keepeth thee will not slumber.

—Psalm 121:3

Thou preparest a table before me in the presence of mine enemies: thou anointest my head with oil; my cup runneth over.

—Psalm 23:5

Wash me throughly
from mine iniquity, and
cleanse me from my sin.

—Psalm 51:2

And they that know thy name will put their trust in thee: for thou, LORD, hast not forsaken them that seek thee.

—Psalm 9:10

O God, be not far
from me: O my
God, make haste
for my help.

–Psalm 71:12

Blessed be the Lord, who daily loadeth us with benefits, even the God of our salvation. Selah.

—Psalm 68:19

The grace of our Lord Jesus Christ be with you. Amen.

–1 Thessalonians 5:28

Behold, God is mine helper:
the Lord is with them that
uphold my soul.
—Psalm 54:4

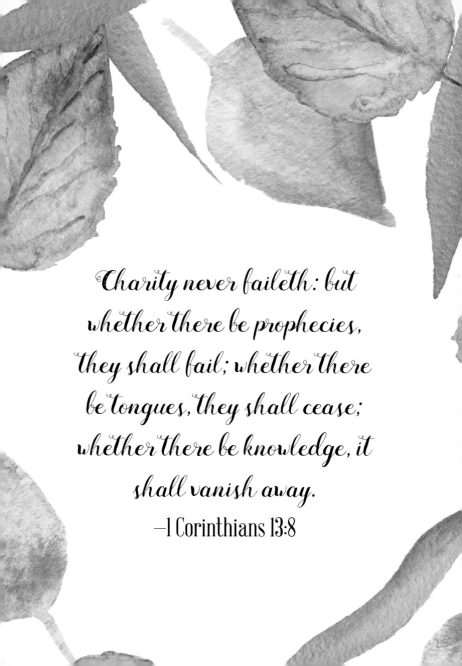

Charity never faileth: but whether there be prophecies, they shall fail; whether there be tongues, they shall cease; whether there be knowledge, it shall vanish away.

—1 Corinthians 13:8

But if we hope for that we see not, then do we with patience wait for it.

—Romans 8:25

But the **LORD** is my defence; and my God is the rock of my refuge.

—Psalm 94:22

Let your conversation be without covetousness; and be content with such things as ye have: for he hath said, I will never leave thee, nor forsake thee.

—Hebrews 13:5

The LORD preserveth the simple: I was brought low, and he helped me.

–Psalm 116:6

But the mercy of the LORD is from everlasting to everlasting upon them that fear him, and his righteousness unto children's children . . .

—Psalm 103:17

Hear my cry, O God;

attend unto my prayer.

–Psalm 61:1

THE RIGHTEOUS CRY, AND THE LORD
HEARETH, AND DELIVERETH THEM OUT
OF ALL THEIR TROUBLES.

—Psalm 34:17

Jesus said unto him, Thou shalt
love the Lord thy God with all thy
heart, and with all thy soul, and
with all thy mind.

—Matthew 22:37

For the LORD God is a sun and shield: the LORD will give grace and glory: no good thing will he withhold from them that walk uprightly.

—Psalm 84:11

Save me, O God; for the waters are come in unto my soul.

—Psalm 69:1

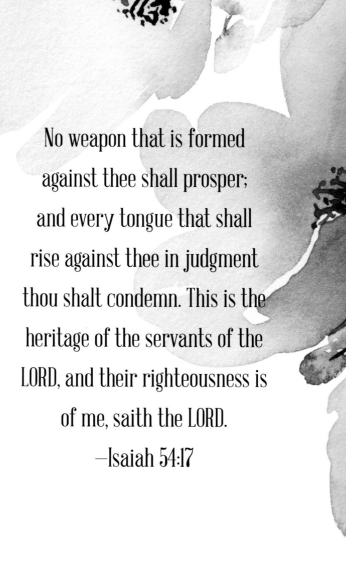

No weapon that is formed
against thee shall prosper;
and every tongue that shall
rise against thee in judgment
thou shalt condemn. This is the
heritage of the servants of the
LORD, and their righteousness is
of me, saith the LORD.
—Isaiah 54:17

O God, thou knowest my foolishness; and my sins are not hid from thee.

—Psalm 69:5

I sought the Lord, and he heard me,
and delivered me from all my fears.

–Psalm 34:4

We know that whosoever is born of God sinneth not; but he that is begotten of God keepeth himself, and that wicked one toucheth him not.

–1 John 5:18

Why art thou cast down,
O my soul? and why art
thou disquieted within me?
hope thou in God: for I shall
yet praise him, who is the
health of my countenance,
and my God.

—Psalm 42:11

Though I walk in the midst of trouble, thou wilt revive me: thou shalt stretch forth thine hand against the wrath of mine enemies, and thy right hand shall save me.

—Psalm 138:7

And hide not thy face
from thy servant; for
I am in trouble: hear
me speedily.

—Psalm 69:17

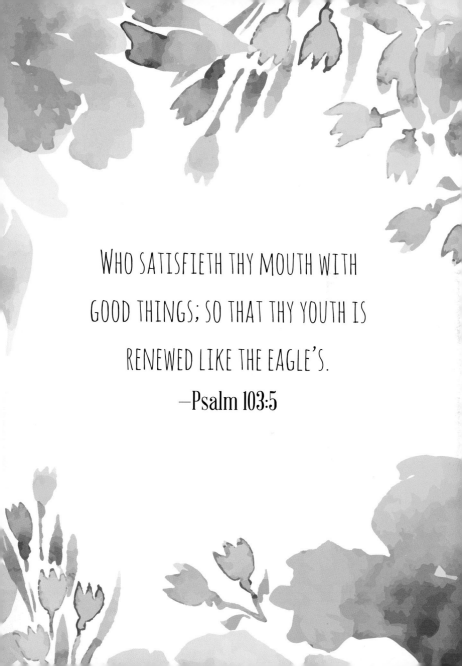

WHO SATISFIETH THY MOUTH WITH
GOOD THINGS; SO THAT THY YOUTH IS
RENEWED LIKE THE EAGLE'S.

—Psalm 103:5

Blessed are the merciful: for they shall obtain mercy.

—Matthew 5:7

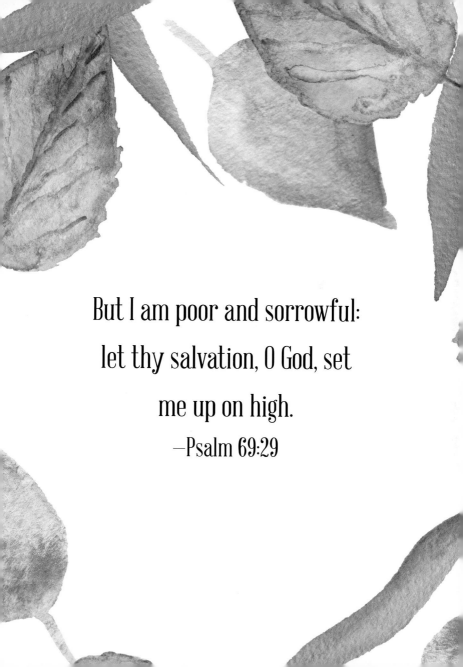

But I am poor and sorrowful:
let thy salvation, O God, set
me up on high.

—Psalm 69:29

O Lord, our Lord, how excellent is thy name in all the earth! who hast set thy glory above the heavens.

—Psalm 8:1

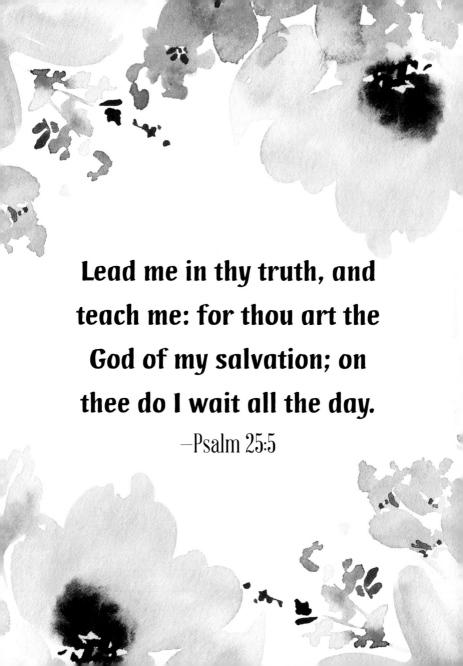

Lead me in thy truth, and teach me: for thou art the God of my salvation; on thee do I wait all the day.

–Psalm 25:5

Truly my soul waiteth upon God: from him cometh my salvation.

—Psalm 62:1

And because ye are sons,
God hath sent forth the
Spirit of his Son into your
hearts, crying, Abba, Father.

–Galatians 4:6

Grace and peace be multiplied
unto you through the knowledge of
God, and of Jesus our Lord . . .
–2 Peter 1:2

For I know the thoughts that I think toward you, saith the **LORD**, thoughts of peace, and not of evil, to give you an expected end.

–Jeremiah 29:11

The spirit of God hath
made me, and the breath
of the Almighty hath
given me life.

—Job 33:4

But now, O LORD, thou art our father;

we are the clay, and thou our potter;

and we all are the work of thy hand.

—Isaiah 64:8

Then shall we know,
if we follow on to know
the **LORD**: his going forth
is prepared as the morning;
and he shall come unto us
as the rain, as the latter and
former rain unto the earth.

–Hosea 6:3

The Lord is not slack
concerning his promise, as
some men count slackness; but
is longsuffering to us-ward,
not willing that any should
perish, but that all should
come to repentance.

—2 Peter 3:9

My son, be wise,
and make my
heart glad,
that I may
answer him that
reproacheth me.

–Proverbs 27:11

For all the promises of God
in him are yea, and in him
Amen, unto the glory of
God by us.
—2 Corinthians 1:20

But thou, when thou prayest, enter into thy closet, and when thou hast shut thy door, pray to thy Father which is in secret; and thy Father which seeth in secret shall reward thee openly.

—Matthew 6:6

He that followeth after righteousness and mercy findeth life, righteousness, and honour.

—Proverbs 21:21

Hereby know we that we dwell in him, and he in us, because he hath given us of his Spirit.

—1 John 4:13

And God shall wipe away
all tears from their
eyes; and there shall be
no more death, neither
sorrow, nor crying,
neither shall there be any
more pain: for the former
things are passed away.
—Revelations 21:4

But as it is written, Eye hath not seen, nor ear heard, neither have entered into the heart of man, the things which God hath prepared for them that love him.

–1 Corinthians 2:9

In the multitude of my
thoughts within me thy
comforts delight my soul.

—Psalm 94:19

HUMBLE YOURSELVES THEREFORE
UNDER THE MIGHTY HAND OF
GOD, THAT HE MAY EXALT YOU
IN DUE TIME . . .
—1 Peter 5:6

Being confident of this very thing, that he which hath begun a good work in you will perform it until the day of Jesus Christ . . .

–Philippians 1:6

For the eyes of the LORD run to and fro throughout the whole earth, to shew himself strong in the behalf of them whose heart is perfect toward him.

–2 Chronicles 16:9a

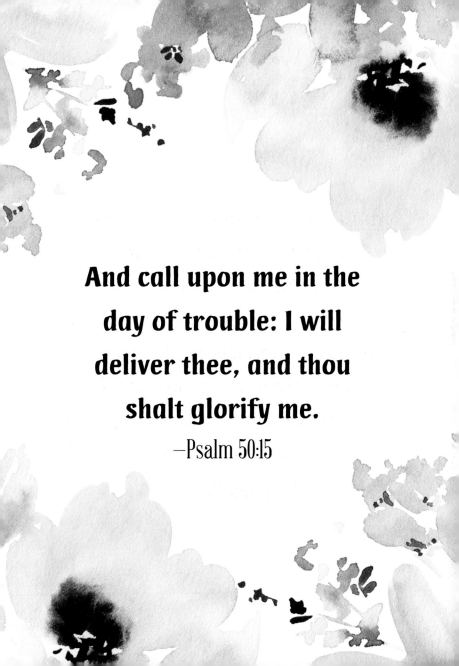

And call upon me in the
day of trouble: I will
deliver thee, and thou
shalt glorify me.

—Psalm 50:15

In whom we have boldness and access with confidence by the faith of him.

—Ephesians 3:12

He giveth power to the faint;
and to them that have no
might he increaseth strength.

—Isaiah 40:29

Honour thy father and
mother; which is the first
commandment with promise...
–Ephesians 6:2

There hath no temptation taken
you but such as is common to
man: but God is faithful, who
will not suffer you to be tempted
above that ye are able; but will
with the temptation also make
a way to escape, that ye may be
able to bear it.

–1 Corinthians 10:13

Trust ye in the LORD for ever: for in the LORD JEHOVAH is everlasting strength

–Isaiah 26:4

Hear counsel, and receive
instruction, that thou mayest be wise
in thy latter end.

—Proverbs 19:20

Yet the LORD will command his lovingkindness in the day time, and in the night his song shall be with me, and my prayer unto the God of my life.

–Psalm 42:8

For all flesh is as grass, and all the glory of man as the flower of grass. The grass withereth, and the flower thereof falleth away: But the word of the Lord endureth for ever. And this is the word which by the gospel is preached unto you.

–1 Peter 1:24-25

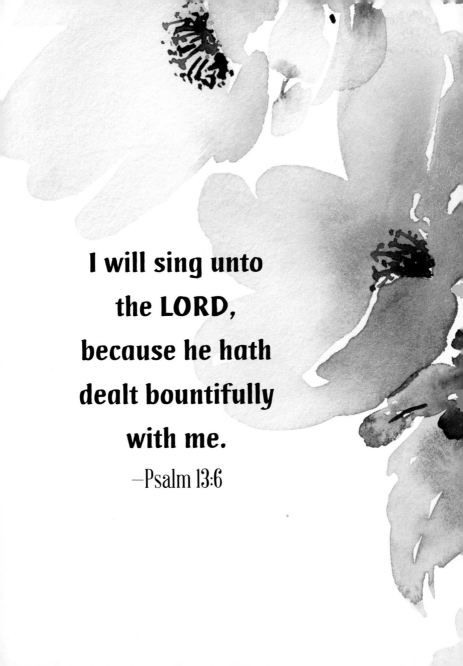

I will sing unto
the **LORD,**
because he hath
dealt bountifully
with me.

–Psalm 13:6

If any of you lack wisdom, let him ask of God, that giveth to all men liberally, and upbraideth not; and it shall be given him.

—James 1:5

Now the God of peace, that brought again from the dead our Lord Jesus, that great shepherd of the sheep, through the blood of the everlasting covenant, Make you perfect in every good work to do his will, working in you that which is wellpleasing in his sight, through Jesus Christ; to whom be glory for ever and ever. Amen.

—Hebrews 13:20-21

For I will pour water upon him that is thirsty, and floods upon the dry ground: I will pour my spirit upon thy seed, and my blessing upon thine offspring . . .

—Isaiah 44:3

God setteth the solitary in families: he bringeth out those which are bound with chains: but the rebellious dwell in a dry land.

—Psalm 68:6

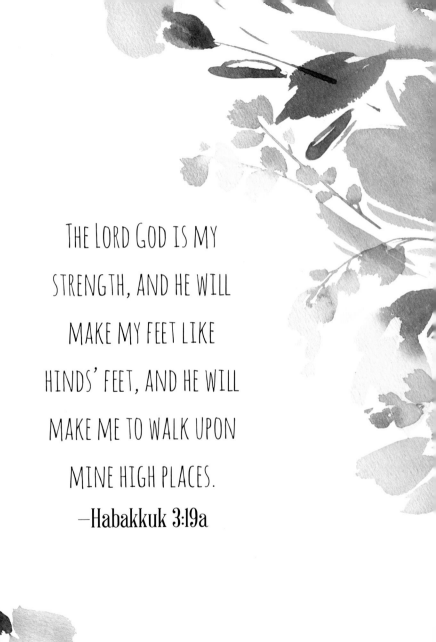

The Lord God is my strength, and he will make my feet like hinds' feet, and he will make me to walk upon mine high places.

—Habakkuk 3:19a

I will call upon the Lord, who is worthy to be praised: so shall I be saved from mine enemies.

—Psalm 18:3

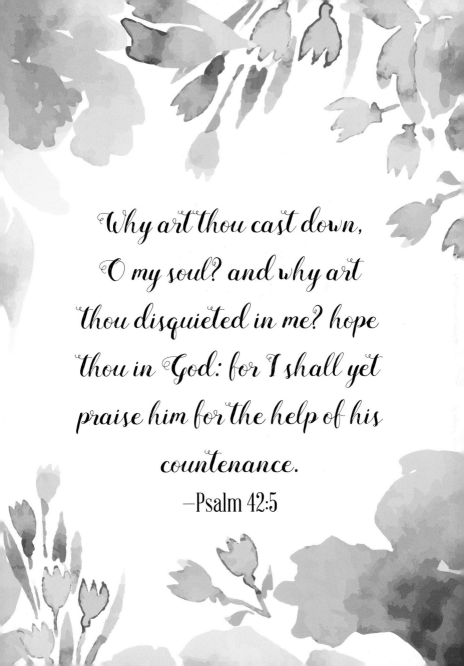

Why art thou cast down,
O my soul? and why art
thou disquieted in me? hope
thou in God: for I shall yet
praise him for the help of his
countenance.

—Psalm 42:5

Blessed are the peacemakers: for they shall be called the children of God.

–Matthew 5:9

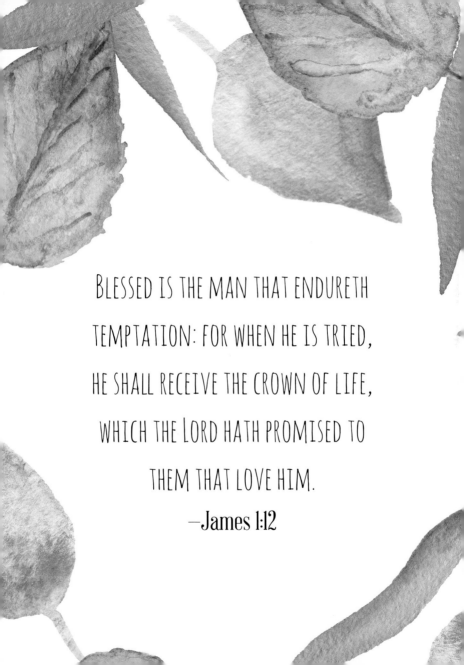

Blessed is the man that endureth temptation: for when he is tried, he shall receive the crown of life, which the Lord hath promised to them that love him.

—James 1:12

Let the words of my mouth, and the meditation of my heart, be acceptable in thy sight, O LORD, my strength, and my redeemer.

—Psalm 19:14

In the fear of the **LORD** is strong confidence: and his children shall have a place of refuge.

–Proverbs 14:26

When I said, My foot slippeth; thy mercy, O Lord, held me up.

—Psalm 94:18

*A father of the fatherless,
and a judge of the widows, is
God in his holy habitation.*

—Psalm 68:5

But I have trusted in thy mercy; my heart shall rejoice in thy salvation.

–Psalm 13:5

Hear the right, O Lord, attend unto
my cry, give ear unto my prayer, that
goeth not out of feigned lips.

—Psalm 17:1

I will love thee, O LORD, my strength.

–Psalm 18:1

The heavens declare the glory of God; and the firmament sheweth his handywork.

–Psalm 19:1

Some trust in chariots, and some in horses: but we will remember the name of the LORD our God.

–Psalm 20:7

But thou art he that took me out of the womb: thou didst make me hope when I was upon my mother's breasts.

—Psalm 22:9

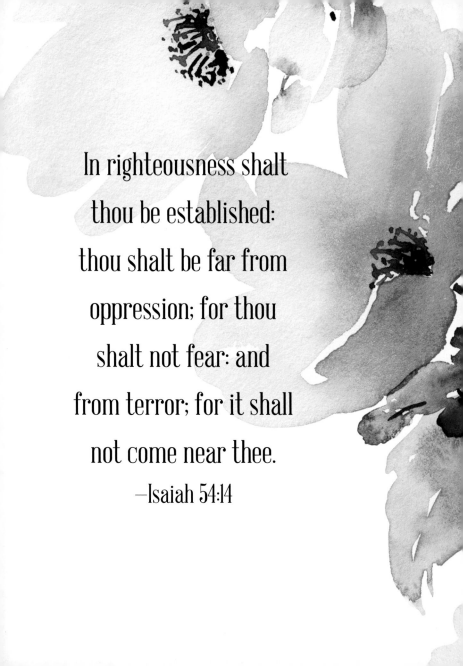

In righteousness shalt thou be established: thou shalt be far from oppression; for thou shalt not fear: and from terror; for it shall not come near thee.

—Isaiah 54:14

As the hart panteth
after the water brooks,
so panteth my soul
after thee, O God.

—Psalm 42:1

O SEND OUT THY LIGHT AND
THY TRUTH: LET THEM LEAD ME;
LET THEM BRING ME UNTO
THY HOLY HILL, AND TO THY
TABERNACLES.

—Psalm 43:3

In God we boast all the
day long, and praise thy
name for ever. Selah.

–Psalm 44:8

I will make thy name to be remembered in all generations: therefore shall the people praise thee for ever and ever.

—Psalm 45:17

**For this God is our
God for ever and ever:
he will be our guide
even unto death.**

–Psalm 48:14

But I am like a green olive tree in the house of God: I trust in the mercy of God for ever and ever.

—Psalm 52:8